A RIVERS OF THE WORLD BOOK

The Ganges: Sacred River of India

BY VIOLET WEINGARTEN

ABOUT THE BOOK: This story of the 1,500-mile-long Ganges River, from her source to the sea and from old times to the present, tells the story of India's civilization and culture. Among the many topics covered in this informative study are the Hindu religion, the background of the caste system, brief biographies of many of India's great religious and political leaders, and the Ganges' role in the past and in the modern world. This is part of Garrard's RIVERS OF THE WORLD series, designed to provide an interesting approach to history, geography, and social studies, and to show young readers how the world's great rivers have influenced the land and man's way of life.

Subject classification: Social Studies, Comparative and Intercultural Studies
Sub-classification: Indian History and Georgraphy, Information

ABOUT THE AUTHOR: Violet Weingarten was born in San Francisco and grew up in New York City. After graduating from Cornell University, she worked as a newspaper reporter. Her assignments included everything from royal visits and murder trials to bagpipe-playing concerts. Now she works with her husband in their public relations office. She has written innumerable pamphlets as well as the scripts for several prize-winning motion pictures produced by Mr. Weingarten. This is Mrs. Weingarten's third book for Garrard, following two other RIVERS OF THE WORLD BOOKS: *The Nile* and *The Jordan*.

Reading Level: Grade 5   Interest Level: Grades 4–7
96 pages . . . 6⅞ x 9⅛   Publisher's Price: $2.32
SBN 8116-6372-8

Illustrated with photographs; reinforced binding; index

GARRARD PUBLISHING COMPANY

Calogero Cascio from Rapho Guillumette

RIVERS OF THE WORLD

THE
Ganges
SACRED RIVER OF INDIA

by VIOLET WEINGARTEN

Map by Henri Fluchere

GARRARD PUBLISHING COMPANY
CHAMPAIGN, ILLINOIS

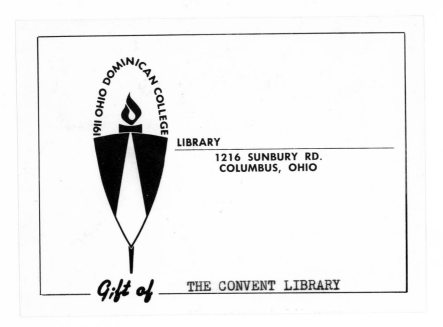
For reading the manuscript of this book and checking the accuracy of its content, the author and publisher are grateful to Dr. David Rubin, Sarah Lawrence College.

United Nations

Contents

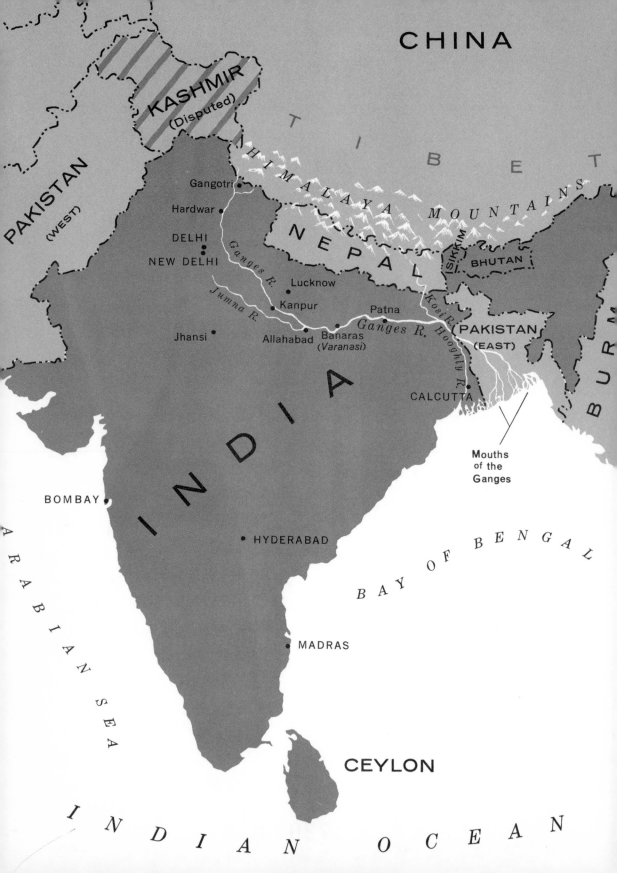

1. Mother Ganges

Once long ago, the Indians say, the Ganges River was a goddess named Ganga. Her father was a king, and her mother, a nymph named Mena.

She first came to earth to help the souls of 60,000 Indian princes get into heaven. The princes were brothers who had been burned to death by a holy man they had insulted. Unless their souls were freed of sin, the princes would have to go to hell. So Ganga turned herself into a river and washed their sins away.

Indians who practice the Hindu religion still worship the Ganges as a goddess. It is the holiest river on earth. The Ganges stretches 1,500 miles from its source in the world's highest mountains, the icy Himalayas, to its ten mouths at the Bay of Bengal. Hindus consider every drop of water along the way sacred.

Hindus call the great yellow river "Ganga Ma," or Mother Ganges. They drink it, bathe in it, carry its water in bottles to far-off villages for those who cannot visit the river themselves. The dearest wish of every Hindu is to die near the Ganges so that his body may be burned on its bank and his ashes thrown into its waters. If that is done, he believes, his soul will be freed of sin, just as the souls of the ancient princes were. Even saying the name of the Ganges aloud is supposed to bring good fortune.

For thousands of years people have been making pilgrimages to the Ganges. Even though they stay strictly separate elsewhere, princes and beggars, learned men and the poorest of peasants wash in the river side by side. Millions throng to bathe

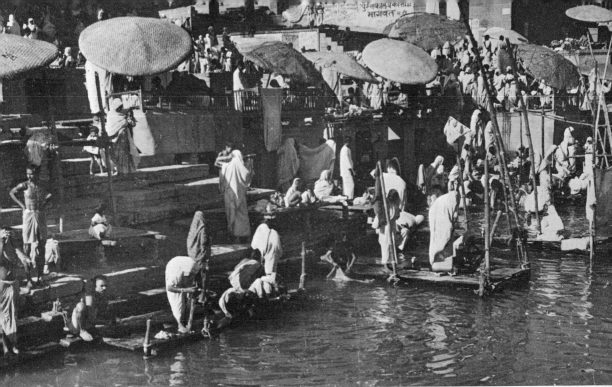

Pilgrims to the holy city of Banaras bathe in the sacred Ganges. Priests are seated under the straw umbrellas.

at the same time. Often they are diseased, for Hindus believe the Ganges has the power to heal sickness. Cattle, which are considered sacred in India, wade in the river at will. Sanitation is usually very poor in the villages and cities along its banks. Yet Ganges water is surprisingly pure. It cleanses itself quickly as it courses. In the days of sailing ships, sailors liked to fill their holds from the Ganges. It stayed fresher longer than the water from other rivers.

The Ganges is a river of glaring contrasts.

At its source in the snowy mountains, it is possible to ski. In the lowlands where it reaches the sea, temperatures reach as high as 120 degrees.

Over five million people live in Calcutta, one of the great cities on the river, yet most of the inhabitants of the Ganges plain live in tiny villages.

In the busy streets of Calcutta, automobiles and streetcars compete for space with rickshaws pulled by hand.

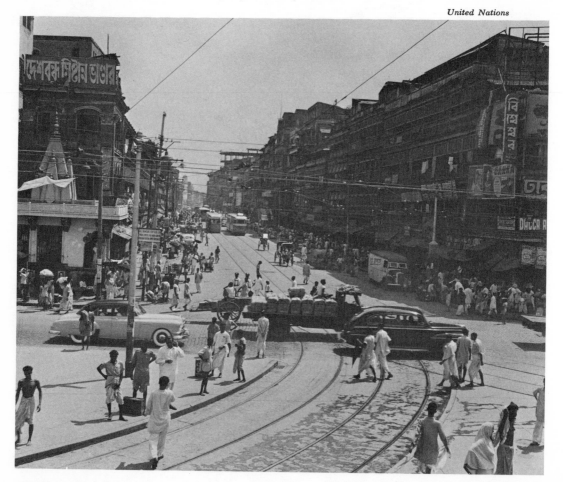

On the Ganges plain farmers and their families live in thatched-roof huts in little villages.

Gold-encrusted temples stand beside mud huts where children starve.

Stone Age tools may be found in the river mud near sites where modern dams are rising to control the river and its tributaries.

One of the world's oldest civilizations developed on the Ganges plain. But geologically the area is one of the youngest on the earth's surface. Geologists believe it was a shallow sea until about 200,000 years ago when the Himalayas pushed through the earth's crust, causing the waters to fall back and the great plain to form.

People have always crowded into the Ganges plain because its soil is the richest in the world. Yet its inhabitants are among the poorest on earth.

The Ganges has always been a highway for conquest. The soldiers of ancient Greece, Scythians, White Huns, Afghans, Mongols, Persians, Turks, Arabs, the Portuguese, Dutch, French, and British came over sea and mountain to conquer and rule. But no army ever completely broke the spirit of the people of the Ganges plain.

Three of the world's important religions— Hinduism, Buddhism, and Jainism—developed beside the Ganges. Great universities flourished there before Europe had any centers of learning.

The last quarter of a century has been one of the most important periods in India's long history. For the first time in more than 700 years, India became free of foreign rule. And the center of India's fight for that independence was the Ganges plain. No wonder India's first prime minister, Jawaharlal Nehru, said, "The story of the Ganga, from her source to the sea, from old times to new, is the story of India's civilization and culture."

2. The Locks of Shiva

High in the peaks of the Himalayas there is a mountain cave, dripping with icicles.

The icicles are the matted locks of the god Shiva, Hindus believe. They say the locks were frozen when Shiva offered to let the goddess Ganga fall into India by dividing into streams through his hair. Otherwise, he was afraid, the force of the rushing water would drown the people below.

Another god, Bhagirathi, showed Ganga the way into India. He can be seen to this day, too, in a small head stream at the river source and in a tributary near Calcutta. Both are named Bhagirathi.

Hindus trudge through the snowy Himalayas to pray to the goddess Ganga in Gangotri.

Fed by melting snow, the Ganges drops from the Himalayan mountain cave to the little town of Gangotri. Here, 10,000 feet up in the sky, there is a temple in honor of the goddess Ganga. Pilgrims come through rugged canyon and mountain forest to worship at its shrine.

For 300 miles after it leaves Gangotri, the Ganges tumbles through a deep gorge to the holy city of Hardwar. At one time Hardwar was called Gangadwara, or "Gates of the Ganges." Here the river spills into a network of canals bringing water to farms. One of the highest dams in the world is being built at this point, with the help of the United States. But most of the Ganges still runs free. The sacred waters must not be blocked.

Hardwar is an important place of pilgrimage. No meat may be eaten there because the Hindu religion frowns on animal slaughter. In this part of the river, fish are also considered sacred; many are tame and swim to the surface to be fed by visitors.

After Hardwar the Ganges enters its great plain. Torrents and waterfalls are at an end, and the river turns shallow. Sluggishly it heads toward sea, dropping only a few inches a mile. As far as the eye can see, there is no sign of elevation on either side. The Ganges has always been a wanderer, and the broad flat plain is dotted with inland villages and faded cities that used to be on the river before it changed its course.

The first big city on the plain is the industrial center of Kanpur, the "Pittsburgh" of India.

Next comes Allahabad, named the "City of Allah" by India's Muslims. Hindus call it Prayag, or "place of sacrifice." Here the Ganges, brown with mud and silt, picks up the first of its many tributaries, the blue Jumna River. Hindus consider the sand bank where the two rivers meet, the holiest spot on earth. The ashes of Prime Minister Nehru and Mohandas Gandhi, India's most revered leader, were thrown into the Ganges here.

Each January a religious fair called the *Magh Mela* takes place at Allahabad. Every twelve years when the sun, the moon, and the stars are in the zodiacal sign of Aquarius the Water Bearer, a particularly large fair called the *Kumbh Mela* is held. Bathing in the river then is supposed to bring so much good luck that no one can count it.

During the most recent *Kumbh Mela*, some twelve million people poured into the city. Several

Millions of the Hindu faithful set up housekeeping in Allahabad for the sacred fair of Kumbh Mela.

million of the pilgrims waded into the river at the start of the celebration.

For days before a *mela*, pilgrims arrive on foot, by boat, cart, donkey, bicycle, bus, special train, or even airplane. A great tent city is set up on the sandy flats between the Jumna and the Ganges. Families cook over open fires. Flags and pennants fly everywhere from long poles. Priests mark the bodies of worshippers with colored dyes. Bells and gongs sound day and night. Beside the water, barbers squat, shaving heads of male bathers and cutting women's hair short. Small children get lost, sacred cows knock over tents, dogs bark.

Everyone rises before sunrise to go to the chilly river with offerings of incense, marigolds, and milk. They may be trampled in the huge crowd, but pilgrims accept the risk gladly. And no matter how jammed the river may be, everyone worships with dignity, rejoicing that his dream of bathing in the Ganges at a sacred time has come true.

Banaras, which the Indians call Varanasi, is the

Stone steps descend to the Ganges in the ancient city of Banaras.

next great city on the river's journey. Possibly it is the oldest city in the world to have been continuously inhabited. It is certainly one of the most important places of pilgrimage in India. A thousand gilded temples, palaces, and *ghats*, or stone landings and steps leading to the water, stretch along the shore for four miles. All day long, smoke floats over the river from the special *ghats* where mourners come to burn the crimson-, white-, or yellow-wrapped bodies of their loved ones.

Next comes Patna, built over the ruins of Pataliputra, a city famous throughout Asia for a thousand years. Four centuries before the time of Christ, it was a great trading center known as Lotus City. Now all that is left of its great heritage are some ancient place names.

Below Patna the Ganges is joined by the Kosi River, which used to flood regularly when the snows melted in the Himalayas. Farms, huts, animals, and people used to be washed away. A new dam helps control the river now. After Patna comes the last city on its journey, Calcutta, where the Ganges gets a new name, the Hooghly.

In the shadow of Calcutta's modern Howrah Bridge, the poor and the faithful share the riverbank with the city's sacred cows.

Calcutta is the largest city of India and among the largest cities in the world. It was India's capital until the government moved to New Delhi in 1912. Everything about Calcutta is extreme. It has the third largest cantilever bridge ever built, over which pass the latest model Rolls-Royce and the most primitive ox cart and rickshaw. The city has the world's biggest university, where 100,000 students are taught in three shifts. Its botanical garden has the world's widest tree, a 200-year-old banyan, with branches spreading to cover a circumference of 1,200 feet of ground. Ocean liners and shallow river boats use the Hooghly. The city is a huge industrial center, a railroad hub, a luxurious tourist spot. Yet many of its inhabitants are so poor they cannot afford homes and must live and die on the streets.

Calcutta is one of the youngest of India's cities, founded by the British in 1690 as a makeshift town for trading with the Portuguese. Each year when the Portuguese galleys sailed home again, the jungle took over. There were other dangers too. Each night a heavy chain had to be stretched across the river to keep out the fast shallow boats of river pirates from Burma.

Two river boats unload their cargoes in the busy port of Calcutta.

3. Cyclones and Crocodiles

The pirates who chased the Portuguese galleys up the Ganges to Calcutta made the jagged coast at the Bay of Bengal their headquarters. There were so many that for hundreds of years every shore city had a fortified wall around it.

The river is still dangerous from Calcutta to the bay, 86 miles away. But today the menace is not from pirates, but from shoals, sandbars, and shifting currents. Forty percent of India's exports go abroad by freighter from Calcutta, and each ship must have a special pilot for the treacherous journey to the sea.

The Ganges reaches the Bay of Bengal through the world's largest delta, dividing into ten mouths, or streams, and into dozens of smaller rivulets. The triangle-shaped delta stretches 200 miles from west to east.

Its most westerly mouth, the one that leads from Calcutta to the sea, is still called the Hooghly as it meets the sea at Sagar Island. The island swarms with crocodiles. Long ago, the story goes, the people of Sagar Island had no water, because of a curse. The goddess Ganga divided herself into a hundred channels to get water to them, and that is how the great delta was formed.

The most easterly mouth of the Ganges is called the Meghna. It is in East Pakistan, which used to be part of India before India became independent. Here the river is joined by the Brahmaputra, bearing water from the mountains of Assam, which has the heaviest rainfall on earth. In flood time the combined rivers pour out 1,800,000 cubic feet of water per second, more than the mighty Mississippi at the height of its flood.

The great Pakistan jungle forest known as the Sunderbans, or "beautiful forest," lies in the middle of the delta. For mile upon mile the jungle

Ylla from Rapho Guillumette

Elephants lift huge logs easily in the forests of East Pakistan.

is so thick the sun barely shines through. Until recent times there were tigers on the Ganges plain. There are still tigers in the Sunderbans, as well as sharks, crocodiles, huge bats, pythons, monkeys, and wild boars.

There are elephants too, but most of them are tame. They work as loggers in the teakwood forests. Farmers in the delta plant teak seedlings in rice paddies in order to give them a good start in the warm Ganges water. Then they transplant them to the forest.

Rice paddies like these are a common sight on the Ganges delta.

The Ganges is a farmer's river from start to finish, despite its glamorous cities. Eighty-five percent of its 500,000-square-mile basin, twice the size of Texas, is rural. Most of the world's supply of jute, the tough reed whose fibers make the best twine or burlap, comes from the Ganges delta. Rice is another important delta crop. In the plains above the delta, fields stretch to the horizon on both sides of the river. Rice grows here too, along with sugar cane, wheat, and pulses, or peas.

Farm life revolves around the monsoon, the season of heavy rainfall.

In the delta, beset by constant cyclones, the monsoon isolates villages. Tidal waves, four to eight feet high, flood roads and bridges, so that river boats are the only means of transportation. Villages are built on rises or man-made mounds of earth, but in some years even these are washed away by torrential rains. All the same the rains mean life in the delta, so they are welcomed.

The monsoon season is also an anxious time up river on the plain. If the rains are too heavy, there is danger of flood. If the rains are too light, there is famine.

Only a few thatched roofs and the top of a car can be seen in this village after a heavy monsoon rain.

Black Star

These water buffalo, resting on a hot day, are used to plow fields.

A good monsoon is like the coming of spring in the United States, a time of new grass, flowers, singing birds, and new crops.

Unlike the delta, where it is always hot, the plain has three seasons. From October to February the weather is mild, except for an occasional freezing spell. Usually, under a soft blue sky, bright birds—mynahs, velvety crows, kites, bulbuls, kingfishers, parakeets, hoopoes—dip into the river. Cattle lie in the shallows, crocodiles sun themselves on floating logs, monkeys chatter in the groves, snakes slither through the reeds. Trees flower with great pink, gold, lavender, and scarlet blossoms that are reflected in the water.

At the end of February, the weather becomes much warmer. In March the *loo*, a hot dry wind, blows. Then, as weeks go by, the fields dry up and the weather turns stifling. Village lanes turn to dust. Birds hide, and animals and humans pant for water.

Then all of a sudden, sometime in June when it seems as if no one can bear the heat or the dust a moment longer, the wind roars, the skies open up. It is the monsoon. Everyone rushes outside, eager to get soaked. The pouring rain is a promise of life itself.

A gibbon, the smallest ape, uses its long arms to swing from trees.

Ylla from Rapho Guillumette

4. Land of the Aryans

About 3,000 years ago, there was a great war between the Kurus and their cousins, the Pandavas, for the rule of two kingdoms along the Ganges.

As the vast Hindu epic poem called the *Mahabharata* tells the story, the war ended in a battle in which almost all participants were killed. Only a Pandava named Yudhishthira, Yudhishthira's wife, and his four brothers survived.

Thereafter Yudhishthira ruled the Ganges kingdoms for fifteen years. Then with his wife, his brothers, and his faithful dog, he journeyed to heaven. One by one, each died until only the king and his dog were left. The god Indra appeared in a chariot and invited Yudhishthira to go to heaven with him. The king began to put his dog in the chariot, but Indra said there was no place for the dog in heaven.

"In that case," said the king, "I won't go either."

Indra was so pleased to see his loyalty that he relented and agreed to let the animal in. To this day, it is said, Yudhishthira's dog is the only dog in heaven.

The people described in the *Mahabharata* were the Aryan ancestors of the present-day Hindus. They began to come through the passes of the Himalayas from Central Asia about 2,000 B.C. Earlier civilizations had already existed in India for thousands of years. When the light-skinned Aryans struggled past the high mountains, driving their cattle before them, they found descendants of at least two peoples, dark-skinned Dravidians and brown-skinned Mediterraneans.

Other Aryans were to go to the west. Some reached as far as Ireland. The name Eire, for Ireland, goes back to these Aryans. The Aryans who came to India sought pasture for their cattle.

After this boy performs the sacred thread ceremony with his father, he will be a member of one of the three highest castes.

Some scholars believe that Hindus still consider cattle sacred because their ancestors valued their animals so highly. Their very word for "war" was "desire for more cows." Over the centuries the Aryans mingled with the people living on the plain and introduced many of their own ways, especially their language and unique caste system.

The language the Aryans brought is called Sanskrit. It is the basis of the main languages of the Ganges plain, and for some of the 845 other languages and dialects spoken throughout India today. Many European languages, including English, go back to the same parent Indo-European language; words spoken near the Ganges might sound quite familiar to us. For instance, the Hindu word for "mother" is *mata*, from the Sanskrit word *matri*.

The caste system of the Aryans divided people into four classes—priests, soldiers, merchants, and peasants, or workers. Beneath these four groups were people who had no caste. In time they came to be known as "untouchables."

The caste system became very complicated.

It is not likely that these women laborers will ever be able to change their occupation or their caste.

Today, while "untouchables" no longer exist by law, there are still about 19,000 different castes and sub-castes in India.

According to Hindu belief everyone is born into a particular caste and remains there for the rest of his life. His caste determines where a man lives, the work he does, the girl he marries, even the people with whom he may eat.

This belief in caste explains, in part, why Hindus feel as they do about the power of the river

Ganges. For they also believe that everyone who dies is born again. If he dies free of sin, he has a good chance of being born into a higher caste. Since the Ganges has the power to wash away sin, the river quite literally is a river of salvation, a path to a better life.

However, there have always been Hindus who did not believe that men were doomed to live according to their caste.

One of these men grew up beside the Ganges nearly 2,500 years ago.

Many Indians hope that, as more children go to school, caste differences will disappear.

Marilyn Silverstone from Magnum

A painting of Buddha
in the Caves of Ajanta.

Government of India Tourist Office, New York

5. The Buddha at Banaras

Siddhartha Gautama, who was to become the Buddha, or the Enlightened One, was born in the foothills of the Himalayas near the source of the Ganges about 500 years before the birth of Jesus. He was the son of a king who brought him up in princely luxury, with a different palace for each season of the year.

Gautama was the king's only son. When he was born, a wise man predicted that one day the boy

34

would see four signs showing the misery of life and from that time on would decide to be not a ruler but a teacher of men. The king tried to prevent this prophecy from coming true. He gave orders that Gautama never be allowed outside the palace grounds.

When Gautama became a young man, however, he stepped through the palace gates and before anyone could stop him, he came upon a sick man, an old man, and a dead man. He was deeply shocked. Later he saw a wandering holy man with no possession other than a begging bowl. This, the fourth sign, made him decide that he, too, must go out into the world without possessions to discover why there should be so much unhappiness everywhere.

That night while everyone in the palace, including his young wife and newborn son, was asleep, Gautama stole away. For six years he wandered along the shores of the Ganges. Each day he begged for only as much food as he could hold in the palm of his hand. Finally he looked like a walking skeleton.

But he was still no closer to understanding the reasons for human misery than when he left his father's palace. He decided that fasting was useless. He sat down under a fig tree, ate some rice a farmer's daughter brought him, and vowed not to stir until he found some answer to his search.

At first gods and spirits surrounded him. Then devils appeared. They told him his family had been hurt. They attacked him with scorn, flood, and earthquake. They sent beautiful women to tempt him and offered him all the power in the world. Still Gautama was unmoved.

At the end of seven weeks, the answer suddenly came to him. It was so simple that he could not understand why he had not thought of it before. Good comes from good deeds, and evil comes from bad deeds. The Hindu religion, which he had learned as a boy, taught that. But if the law of life was that good came from good, and bad from bad, then prayers to gods could not change anything. They were useless. Caste made no sense either. The only difference between people was whether they behaved well or badly. All people were born equal because they all had the same opportunity to choose how they would act.

From that time on, Gautama was known as the Buddha. He sat seven weeks more, thinking. He decided that men suffer because they are not content to do good, but want wealth and power as well. So the way to find peace of mind was to give up worldly desires. Then the Buddha rose and went along the Ganges shore to the holy city of Banaras. He gathered followers in a park where deer were kept, and there he preached his first sermon.

Men, he said, should not live for pleasure, but they should not make themselves miserable either. They should follow a Middle Way, heeding Four Noble Truths and a Noble Eightfold Path. They should not kill, steal, lie, or do anything else they might later be ashamed of. They should be calm, strive always to do good, and keep away from evil and wrong-doing.

Before long the Buddha had many followers. He traveled all over India, teaching. Sometimes as many as 1,200 men and women went along with him. Once a woman came to him with a dead child in her arms and asked him how she could bear her loss. The Buddha told her to bring him a mustard seed from a house where no one had ever died, and then he would help her. She could not, of course, and in that way she learned she was not alone in her sorrow. She, too, became one of the Buddha's followers.

On one occasion the Buddha returned to visit his family. While he was there, a jealous cousin set a raging elephant in his path; when the elephant saw the Buddha, it simply bowed before him. By the time the Buddha left, his wife and many of his relatives had become his followers too.

The Buddha preached for 45 years. At the age of 80, he became ill and knew he would die soon. His followers wept, but the Buddha reminded them that they had his teachings for comfort. "Work out your salvation with diligence," he reminded them, and then he died.

The Buddha and his followers rejected many ideas of Hinduism. But they took for granted that everyone would be reborn repeatedly until he lived

Buddha and his followers spread the new religion throughout India.

such a good life that he reached a state called Nirvana, a joyous nonexistence. The Buddha reached Nirvana when he died, his followers believed. Before that, they said, the Buddha had lived 530 times. Sometimes he had been an animal like the ones they saw along the Ganges, a monkey perhaps, or a deer, or a lion, according to their writings. And whatever animal he had happened to be, he had been, of course, wise and witty.

The Buddha's followers made up some cheerful little stories about these earlier animal lives of the Buddha. They called them the *Jatakas*.

One tells of a monkey king who lived in a forest "near a curve in the Ganges River." He enjoyed eating figs, the fruit of the very tree under which the Buddha became the "Enlightened One." A crocodile's wife told her husband she must have that monkey's heart. Accordingly the crocodile tried to lure the monkey away from the shore. He asked him why he ate only figs when there were so many other good things growing on the other side of the river.

The followers of Buddha's principles today may worship at Buddgaya, a sacred center of Buddhism.

"Because I can't swim," said the monkey king.

"Jump on my back then," said the crocodile, "and I'll take you across."

When they got to the middle of the river, the crocodile started to dive under the water.

"Hey," said the monkey, "if you do that, I'll drown."

When the crocodile explained that was just what he had in mind and told him why, the monkey said he didn't have his heart with him. "I left it on the fig tree," said the monkey, pointing to a branch. "Take me back and I'll get it for you."

The crocodile turned around. As soon as they neared the shore, the monkey leaped to the bank and fled into the woods. Who was the monkey king? Why, none other than the clever Buddha, of course.

With the spread of Buddhism, these stories spread too. Many of them may seem familiar. The reason is that the *Jataka* stories were based on older Indian fables which seem to have a common source with the fables of ancient Greece and other countries. In various forms these fables have been told and retold in Europe and the United States. It is possible to see traces of their Indian origin because many are about Indian, not European, animals. So children all over the world grow up knowing and loving stories told beside the Ganges long years ago.

6. The Ganges Kingdoms

While the Buddha was trying to teach men to stop striving for power and wealth, the Ganges plain was divided into many little countries, each one fighting to take over the other.

A king named Chandragupta Maurya finally won control of the entire plain in the fourth century B.C. His own kingdom was near the mouth of the Ganges. He extended it all the way to the Himalayas. His capital, Pataliputra, stretched along the Ganges for nine miles. It had 64 gates and 570 towers. The walls of the royal palace were covered with gold and silver. When Chandragupta appeared in public, he rode on an elephant in a procession with floats of caged lions and leopards. He was greatly hated because of his cruelty. So many people wanted to kill him, he slept in a different bedroom every night to avoid them.

Chandragupta's grandson Asoka at first was as cruel a ruler as his grandfather. He waged many wars and tortured all who opposed him. Then a saintly Buddhist who did not flinch under his torture converted him to Buddhism. Asoka had just conquered a people named the Kalingas in a particularly bloody war. He took a good look at the misery his war had caused and returned their kingdom to the Kalingas, apologizing for the death and destruction he had wrought.

Asoka made Buddhism the state religion of India, but he was tolerant of all religions. He became a vegetarian, giving up his favorite dish, roast peacock. He tried to spread the peaceful teachings of the Buddha among all men, sending his own son and daughter abroad as good-will ambassadors. To make sure everyone knew about his change of heart, he had his words of peace and kindness carved on rocks and pillars throughout the country. They were written in local dialects so that everyone could understand them. A few

A small fence protects a pillar of Asoka standing at Vaishali.

of Asoka's thousand or so pillars stand beside the Ganges to this very day. India's national emblem is Asoka's lion column at Sarnath, near Banaras.

Asoka's kingdom broke up when he died, and for some six centuries thereafter foreigners invaded the Ganges plains. Then, around A.D. 320, a new king established himself in Asoka's Pataliputra and made it one of the most beautiful cities in the world. He called himself Chandragupta, after Asoka's grandfather. For about a century he and his descendants restored the kingdom to its old glory. But it, too, declined.

In A.D. 606 a king named Harsha took power along the Ganges. Like Asoka, he was a merciful ruler and respected all religions. Harsha was particularly hospitable. He provided free food and lodging for travelers on every highway and had doctors treat them without fee.

From the time of Chandragupta to the time of Harsha, many Chinese scholars visited India to study Buddhism. Some of their diaries and letters still exist. They described the tigers, lions, and wild elephants in the thick jungles on the banks of the Ganges. They said that "in the Ganges Valley, the people are numerous and happy." Harsha was so kind a king, the scholars reported, that he did not believe in beheading. He only had hands chopped off for lawbreaking.

Ancient Indians never made a point of writing down their history; much of our knowledge of their civilization comes from the reports of those Chinese travelers. At Nalanda, a university with 10,000 students near Pataliputra, doctors studied medicine and surgery, especially plastic surgery. Indian mathematicians first worked out the principle of the zero, which they called *shunya*, or nothing. Without the idea of zero, the decimal system and higher mathematics could not exist. The so-called Arabic numerals, which replaced complicated Roman numerals, got to the Arabs from India. The Arabs called mathematics *hindisat*, which means "the Indian art."

Even before the time of Harsha, ships were sailing down the Ganges to the coast, returning

These boatmen are taking their primitive craft downriver much as their ancestors did in Harsha's time.

with gems and spices. The Indian ships went as far as the Mediterranean with musk, saffron, and yak tails from the foothills of the Himalayas, silks and muslins from Bengal, iron from Bihar, and monkeys and parrots from the delta. They also carried a new game called chess and a newly tamed wild fowl called chicken.

Harsha was the last Hindu monarch to rule over a united northern India and the Ganges plain. After waves of invasions by Muslims, followers of the Islamic religion founded in Arabia during the time of Harsha, a Muslim kingdom was established at Delhi. Eventually the whole of the Ganges plain was ruled by Muslim sultans.

In 1398 other Muslims came from Samarkand, a Mongolian kingdom in Central Asia. Their leader, a cruel Tartar prince named Tamerlane, killed so many people at Delhi that he built a pyramid of heads outside the city walls. It is said that not even a bird stirred there for months afterward.

Tamerlane pushed as far as Hardwar on the Ganges. Then he went back to Samarkand with his loot.

7. Babur the Tiger

A century later a 12-year-old descendant of Tamerlane became ruler of Samarkand. When he grew up, he was so warlike he was given the nickname of Babur, which means "tiger" in Persian. First he conquered the chiefs of the Afghan kingdoms near his own Samarkand. He kept a diary in which he described how the chiefs met him with grass between their teeth, meaning, "I am your ox," hoping that he would not kill them.

Later, like Tamerlane, he became curious about the rich land on the other side of the Himalayas. So he fought his way across Central Asia and pushed through the mountain passes into India.

As he approached the Jumna, Hindu princes, who had regained rule of various Indian kingdoms, determined to stop him. They got together an army three times the size of Babur's and assembled at a place called Panipat near Delhi. They put their war elephants at the head of the army, as usual, and waited. The elephants were dressed in leather armor and had metal spikes on their tusks. Each elephant carried two or three soldiers, armed with bows and spears, and a *mahout*, or trainer. Advancing to the sounds of cymbals and trumpets, the elephant troops were a frightening force.

The elephants were easily frightened, themselves. Babur had only 1,200 men on horseback, but he had a weapon neither the Hindus nor their elephants had ever encountered—cannon that fired stones. At the first cannonade, the elephants panicked and ran away, trumpeting loudly. They trampled their own soldiers, and the Hindus were wiped out.

Babur's son Humayun fought at the battle of Panipat. He befriended the family of one of the

Hindu princes killed there, and the grateful family gave him a huge diamond. Humayun presented the diamond to his father. The court jeweler reported it was "worth half the daily expenses of the world." The diamond belonged to India's rulers until 1849, when it was presented to England's Queen Victoria. It is still famous as the Koh-i-Noor diamond.

Unlike Tamerlane, Babur remained in India. There he founded the line of kings known as Moguls, because of their Mongolian origin. Babur was a powerful man. He could ride 80 miles a day on horseback, march 36 miles a day on foot, and swim across the Ganges when it was in full flood. He built many irrigation canals on the Ganges plain. The fields between the Ganges and the Jumna became so fertile their crops fed Babur's entire empire.

After Babur had been ruling for some time, Humayun, then 22, became very ill. Doctors were unable to cure him, so Babur went to see a wise man. "Your son can be saved," the wise man told him. "It is up to you. You must be willing to

Information Service of India, New York

As in Akbar's time, a number of religions exist together in India. Muslims worship at Ajmer (above). A Hindu sits at the entrance of a temple dedicated to the Sun God (right). Worshipers enter a Jain temple (opposite page).

Lynn Millar from Rapho Guillumette

sacrifice the most precious thing in your empire."

Babur knew just what the wise man meant. He vowed to give up his own life if his son got well. His son recovered, and Babur got sick and died.

Humayun was not a great king. But his son Akbar, Babur's grandson, gave India one of the noblest periods in its history. He built up a mighty empire and ruled it justly. He was interested in everything, including different religions, and the more he learned about them, the more tolerant he became.

Like all the Mogul kings, Akbar was a Muslim. But he listened to Buddhist monks with interest. He put dye on his forehead as the Hindus did.

He had enjoyed shooting lions and tigers, but he gave it up at the request of his Jain subjects. The Jains were Indians who were so opposed to killing anything that even today their followers wear gauze masks to avoid breathing in tiny insects.

Akbar's fellow Muslims thought he was going a little too far when he gave up hunting, but the king paid no attention to them. He turned to other interests. He could not read, but he had a library of 24,000 manuscripts, which were read to him. He encouraged art and music. And he played polo. He loved playing polo so much, he invented a luminous ball in order to be able to play it at night. It was made of a kind of wood that smoldered, but did not burn, when it was lit.

His reign covered the last half of the sixteenth century, the same years as that of Queen Elizabeth I of England. He received her ambassadors. His court was always full of travelers. One of these travelers told him what had happened to a man named Columbus, who had been looking for a short cut from Europe to Akbar's kingdom. Columbus

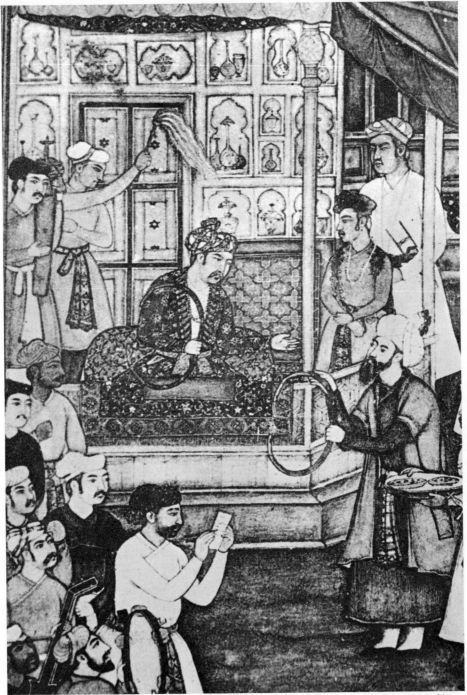

Akbar received these ambassadors from foreign countries in celebration of a military victory.

found a strange new country instead, America.

Meanwhile Europe was getting to know some unusual travelers from India, gypsies. The gypsies originally lived beside the Ganges River. To this day they wear clothes similar to those worn on the banks of the river and speak a language very much like Hindi, one of the chief languages of Northern India. It is thought they were originally members of a caste of Indians called *Doms*, who were musicians and entertainers. Scholars think that the Muslims brought these Indian musicians and dancers with them as they traveled back and forth between India and the Middle East and Europe.

Akbar's kingdom lasted for three more generations, until the early eighteenth century. Then a series of Hindu princes gradually took over the many powers that had been once held by the Mogul kings.

But the riches of the empire built by the great Mogul kings remained, and the new rising class of merchants in Europe began to cast eager eyes toward India.

8. The East India Company

England's merchants got their first foothold in India because Akbar's son Jehangir was devoted to his little daughter. It was the one soft spot in his otherwise cruel heart.

When the little princess became very ill, he was miserable. And when a British sea captain who happened to be at his court produced a medicine that cured her, Jehangir was so grateful he told the captain to ask any reward he wanted.

The captain said he wished his employer, the British East India Company, might establish trading posts in India. Jehangir agreed. The British trading company promptly opened three posts, the biggest one at Calcutta.

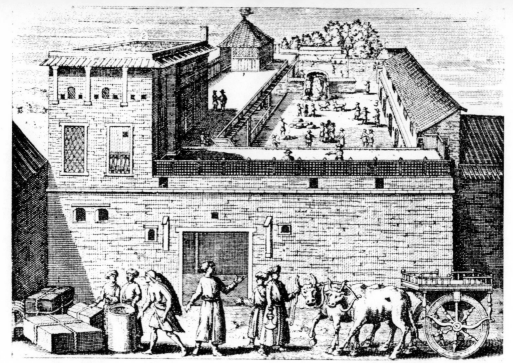

The East India Company's rise to power began at small trading posts like this one.

The trading posts were like small towns, with warehouses, offices, docks, houses, and forts. The East India Company hired its own private army of Indians to guard them. These Indians were called *sepoys*, which is Hindi for "soldiers." The officers were English.

As the power of the East India Company grew, some of the Indian princes tried to resist it. One of the Indian princes opposed to the British company was Siraj-ud-daula, nineteen-year-old grandson of the last Mogul. He attacked the company fort at Calcutta in 1756 during the broiling days just before the monsoon. When he captured the fort, most of its officers and men escaped. Those who remained were jammed into a small airless room overnight; by morning, most were dead. To this day, a stifling small area where many people are crowded may be called "the Black Hole of Calcutta."

The East India Company sent an army of English and Indian soldiers to rescue Calcutta. The army was led by Robert Clive, an Englishman who had started his career as a company clerk. The British forces, about 3,000 men in all, defeated Siraj-ud-daula and his army of 50,000 Indians at nearby Plassey. The young prince fled on a camel.

From that time on, the British were the most important power in India. Within 20 years, so many British came to live in Calcutta alone that the Indian city looked like an English town.

The British government had given the East India Company the rights to buy land in India, to rule whatever territory it acquired, and to make treaties with certain Indian princes. All such

The wealth and splendor amassed by Indian princes during British rule is still in evidence today.

"rights" were in the hands of the East India Company, and were exercised by it, not the British government.

Each year the East India Company became more powerful, setting one Indian ruler against another, hiring Indian troops to fight other Indians, signing treaties in which the company always got the best of the bargain. The company even obtained the right to collect taxes in India.

Most important, perhaps, the East India Company took over India's textile industry. It owned so much of India's cotton acreage that it could decide what became of India's raw cotton. England manufactured cloth by machine. The English company made more money by shipping Indian cotton to England for machine weaving than it would have made had it allowed Indian cotton to be woven by hand in India. Thus it destroyed India's famous hand-weaving industry. Indian weavers lost their jobs. It was said that the banks of the Ganges were covered with the bleached bones of jobless weavers who had died of starvation.

At the same time, British residents in India

With independence has come an effort to rebuild the hand-weaving industry in India.

Troeller from Black Star

were offending Indian pride by their superior attitudes, while many British army officers were treating their Indian troops with cruelty. Indian resentment of the British finally boiled over in the army revolt of 1857, usually called "The Sepoy Mutiny."

The revolt started with Indian soldiers in a barracks near Calcutta. They thought they had been issued cartridges coated with pig fat, considered unclean in both the Hindu and Muslim religions. The soldiers turned against their officers.

The British try to beat back Indian troops in the Sepoy Rebellion.

The revolt soon became more than a military "mutiny." It spread among the people along the entire length of the Ganges plain. Many Indians wanted to win back control of their country from the greedy British company.

The Indians fought hard. They gave no quarter. At Kanpur a Sepoy leader promised not to kill any of the British if they surrendered the town, which a native ruler had ceded to the East India Company. But he broke his word. When the British tried to flee up the Ganges to Allahabad, the Indian troops fired upon them as they huddled in their boats. Only four people were saved.

Farther down the Ganges at the English company's post at Lucknow, some 3,000 men, women, and children were under siege for 87 days. Just when it seemed they could not hold out a moment longer, when they had no more food, water, or able-bodied fighters left, they heard bagpipes in the distance. The pipers were playing "The Campbells Are Coming," and the British thought they were going crazy under the strain. Then the sound came closer, and to their utter amazement, they saw a regiment of Scottish Highlanders, in full kilt uniform, coming to their rescue. A gaunt thousand, all who survived, tottered out of Lucknow to greet the Highlanders.

Indians call the "mutiny" their "First War of Independence." They tell the story of the brave *rani*, or princess, of the small Ganges state of Jhansi. The 20-year-old princess was the widow of the prince of Jhansi. When she learned the British intended to take over her state, she joined the revolution.

The young princess put on a soldier's uniform and rode into battle on horseback. She held the reins in her mouth so she could use both hands to wield the sword, which would have been too heavy for her otherwise. The opposing British did not realize she was a woman, and she was killed in her saddle. The general who fought against her called her the "best and bravest" of the Indian leaders. India considers her its Joan of Arc, and her room in the old fort of Jhansi is a shrine of Indian independence.

Eventually the revolution was suppressed. But

The Tata Iron and Steel Company, established under British rule, is the largest and oldest steel producer in India.

the British people, shocked at the way the East India Company had ruled India, insisted that the company be abolished. The British government took control of India itself. Queen Victoria of England became Empress of India in 1876. India officially became a colony of the British Empire.

Life began to change on the Ganges plain. The British built good roads beside the river and joined its cities by a railroad. They deepened the Ganges channel and put in steamer service as far as Allahabad. They built canals and power plants.

They introduced a common language, English, overcoming the barrier of India's hundreds of different languages and dialects. All these changes made it easier for the English to rule, of course, but they also helped to unify India. And with the English language came the great books and learning of the West, which helped to educate many of the Indians who were to become India's own leaders.

British governors did away with ancient and disturbing Indian customs like child sacrifice and child marriage. They ordered the *suttee ghats* at Banaras closed. These were the stone landings on the Ganges where devout Hindu wives were supposed to kill themselves when their husbands died. Actually very few widows did so any more.

But British rule had its evil side. British insistence that India get its manufactured goods from England destroyed Indian industry. Some craftsmen found work in the cotton and jute mills of Calcutta and other cities, where they lived in miserable shacks. More fled to the little farm villages along the Ganges, where they could at least raise their own food. Eventually, there were so many people living near the river that even in good times its fertile soil could not provide enough food for them.

Then, too, the British did not always practice the justice and democracy they taught. Many of the governors and civil servants sent from England held themselves aloof from the Indians and spoke patronizingly of the "white man's burden." All key positions in the Indian army were held by the British.

Of course, some British admired Indians and treated them as equals. The Indian National Congress, whose members were to fight so hard for India's freedom, was founded by an Englishman. But friendship of a few English people did not make up to the Indian people for India's lack of independence. The Indians did not want merely to hear about freedom; they wanted to have it. And growing up among them was a small boy who would personify this longing. Born seven years before Queen Victoria became Empress of India, he was to become the leader of his country's struggle for independence.

9. River of Freedom

If you did not know who Mohandas Gandhi was, you might have been tempted to laugh at him. He was a toothless skinny little man with dime-store spectacles. Even when he had an appointment with the King of England, he insisted on wearing only the Indian *dhoti*, a simple cotton loincloth. He refused to get false teeth or good clothes because he wanted no more than the poorest peasant in his country could afford.

Gandhi was one of the most remarkable men who ever lived. Born into a high-caste Hindu family, he was married at thirteen, in accordance with the rules of his religion. When he was nineteen, he revolted against caste restrictions. He went to England to study law, even though he would be expelled from his caste for crossing the ocean. After completing his studies, he went to South Africa in 1893. Indian laborers there were being persecuted. Gandhi worked to help the Indians in South Africa over a 21-year span, broken only by brief visits to India. When he finally got back to India to stay in 1914, he vowed to devote the rest of his life to helping his people become free.

Gandi had two kinds of freedom in mind. One was freedom from British rule. The other, equally important, was freedom from the prejudice and backwardness that kept Indians in bondage regardless of their form of government.

He did not propose to use force to achieve either freedom. He still believed the part of the Hindu religion that was opposed to violence. He was also influenced by the ideas of the American writer Henry Thoreau who said that the best way to fight bad laws was simply not to obey them.

Gandhi was a familiar figure among the people of the Ganges plain. The area was the center of the freedom struggle, from Allahabad, headquarters of the Indian National Congress, to Calcutta, site of the Alipore Jail. There, many Indian leaders were imprisoned for long periods for leading protests against the British.

Gandhi's first work in India was among the poor Ganges farmers. He went to Champaran to help the starving sharecroppers who made dyes from indigo. He talked to the pilgrims at Banaras and the huge crowds at the *melas* at Allahabad. At Hardwar one day he told how the Buddha once asked a follower what he had accomplished in three years of meditating beside the Ganges. "I have learned to walk across the surface of the river without getting my feet wet," he said. "Then," replied the Buddha, "you have wasted your time, for there is a ferry just around the corner."

Like the Buddha, Gandhi believed in practical action. He was his own best example. When he wanted people to use hand-woven Indian cloth instead of the cheaper cloth imported from England, he himself got a spinning wheel. Every day he made a point of spinning yarn, thereby showing that there was no shame in handwork, even for people with education. The red, white, and green flag of India has at its center a Buddhist symbol, the wheel of the law, which is often compared to Gandhi's spinning wheel.

Gandhi with his spinning wheel. He encouraged Indians to take pride in the art of hand-weaving.

Wide World

Gandhi was opposed to the caste system which made some people "untouchables." He invited an "untouchable" family to live and eat with his family and followers. He objected to the way dirty work was left to "untouchables." So he and his followers cleaned the outdoor toilets at one of the Allahabad *melas*. Then he renamed the "untouchables." He called them *"harijans,"* which means "children of God."

Under Gandhi's leadership the starving, backward, illiterate people of India gave the greatest demonstration of nonviolent resistance the world has ever seen, against the British Empire at the peak of its power.

When the British put a tax on Indian salt in 1930, Gandhi marched to the sea to get his own salt. He walked for 24 days, gathering millions of followers as he went. When Gandhi finally picked up a lump of sea salt, the police arrested him and 100,000 of the marchers, until they ran out of jail space. The salt marchers spent eight months in prison. Gandhi made no objection. He said he needed "the rest." He was so busy there,

A mounted policeman tries to drive off a crowd of salt marchers.

that he had to have a "Silence Day" once a week to catch up on his mail.

Gandhi and his followers spent years in jail. At one time when he was arrested, Gandhi told the judge he deserved to be jailed for breaking the law. The judge, in turn, told him that if the law could be changed so that Gandhi could be released, "no one will be better pleased than I."

In the autobiography he wrote during another prison stay, Gandhi said that he amused himself guiding bugs from his bed into the office of the English superintendent by means of a tunnel he made from a folded newspaper.

Gandhi often fasted in order to purify himself, in accordance with his belief that nonviolent resisters must be sinless. Gandhi felt that if he and his followers could attain goodness, they could convert the enemy by love, not coercion. When his followers used violence, Gandhi fasted, and they stopped. The British, knowing how precious Gandhi's life was to the Indian people, often made concessions when he went on a hunger strike.

Finally, in 1947, one of Gandhi's dreams came true. The British agreed to grant India its freedom. The great-grandson of Queen Victoria, Viscount Louis Mountbatten, made the transfer of power official.

Gandhi's other dream—that India should be freed of backwardness and intolerance—did not come true as easily. Most Indians were Hindus, but some were Muslims. The Muslims were afraid that a government controlled by Hindus would not give them their rights; they asked to have their own state. Accordingly part of India became the independent state of Pakistan. Half of the Ganges delta, including the Sunderbans jungle, became part of Pakistan. The Ganges plain itself remained Indian. Muslims moved out of villages that were mostly Hindu. Hindus fled from Muslim areas. In all, 8,000,000 people had to leave their homes. There was so much bad feeling that Muslims and Hindus began to kill each other by the hundreds of thousands.

Hindus who have fled Pakistan crowd into New Delhi, setting up their shacks near the fashionable Ashoka Hotel.

Der Stern from Black Star

Gandhi traveled tirelessly along the Ganges plain seeking peace between brothers in the newly established nation.

Heartbroken, Gandhi set out to try to stop the murder. He was 78 years old, but he went the whole length of the Ganges plain, often traveling on foot, to remind people that they should love their fellow men, not hate them. And wherever Gandhi turned up, there was no killing.

In January of 1948 Gandhi went to New Delhi, the capital. He thought the Hindu leaders were behaving unfairly to the Muslims in some ways, and he wanted to persuade them to do better. On January 30 he attended the last of a series of public prayer meetings. He was so frail he had to lean on the shoulders of the two young grand-daughters he lovingly called his "walking sticks." Before Gandhi had a chance to speak, a young Hindu, who thought Gandhi favored the Muslims too much, shot him three times. Gandhi folded his hands, exclaimed, *"He Ram,"* "O God," and died.

One of Gandhi's chief followers, Jawaharlal Nehru, who was then Prime Minister of India, broadcast the sad news over the new All-India Radio. "The light has gone out of our lives," said Nehru.

Gandhi's body was burned beside the Ganges, as he had requested, and his ashes were thrown into the river. There is a park at the spot now, and people from all over the world go there to mourn him.

Gandhi's work was continued by many hands, especially those of Nehru.

Gandhi had inspired Nehru to devote his life to India's freedom. Nehru was the son of Motilal Nehru, a proud and wealthy high-caste Hindu, who owned the first automobile in India. His house near the Ganges was so luxurious it was called the "Abode of Happiness." Young Nehru heard Gandhi speak in 1916 and wanted to join him, but his father forbade it.

Then Gandhi came to the great house at Allahabad and spoke to Motilal. The father was so impressed that he had his entire family join Gandhi's freedom movement. The Nehrus sold or gave away much of their beautiful furniture and works of art, packed up the rest, and moved across the street to a small house. They gave their big house to the Congress Party for its headquarters.

Nehru was jailed nine times by the British. He spent 3,262 days in jail, all told. Once he was released to go to his wife's deathbed. Like Gandhi, he used his time in prison to write books. One of his books describes how he made friends with the squirrels, kittens, and mongooses which found their way into his prison cell. He told how he

Ylla from Rapho Guillumette

Prime Minister Jawaharlal Nehru feeding one of his pet pandas.

used to do a yoga head stand when he was particularly bored. "The slightly comic position increased my good humor," he wrote. One year, he wrote a history of the world for his young daughter Indira.

Nehru remained India's prime minister until he died in 1964. And like Gandhi, his final resting place was the Ganges.

10. Feasts and Holidays

Republic Day, January 26, is a highlight of any Indian prime minister's year. That is the day he reviews the great parade at New Delhi, celebrating India's faith that it would one day be free. Republic Day was proclaimed by the Indian National Congress in 1930 while India was still a colony. Nehru was there when the day of faith was set, and he was India's leader when that faith became fact.

Two years after he died, another Nehru was in the prime minister's box, reviewing the parade. It was his daughter Indira, born in her grandfather's great house near the Ganges, the little girl for whom Nehru had written a history of the world. Indira, now the widow of a man named Gandhi (unrelated to Mohandas Gandhi's family), became a double symbol. Not only was she carrying on her father's work, but she was a living example of India's emancipation. India, recently so backward, had advanced so much that it had a woman prime minister.

So there was a special zest to that 1966 parade. As they do each year, people poured in from the

India's armed forces stride proudly forward in this Republic Day parade in New Delhi.

Marilyn Silverstone from Magnum

Ganges plain and from the hills, wearing colorful costumes and performing the folk dances of their native villages. The parade is always a hodge-podge of ancient and modern India, with jet planes flying overhead, plodding gold-painted army elephants, desert soldiers mounted on camels, and armored tanks. Officials, peasants, people of every color and feature imaginable all join the line of march.

The gayest holidays along the Ganges are the religious festivals. In the Pakistan part of the delta, most holidays are the same as the ones celebrated throughout the Islamic world. But in the rest of the Ganges area, many festivals are linked to seasons important in the life of the farmer.

Holi comes in the spring. It serves two purposes: giving thanks for the winter harvest and letting off steam in the hot dry season. Even the most sober adults enjoy the *Holi* custom of squirting passersby with water colored with red or yellow powder.

When the long-awaited monsoon comes, a holi-

Children wear old clothes when spraying colored water on Holi.

day honors Vishnu, the god of life. It is a way of thanking him for the rain.

The end of the monsoon brings the biggest festival of the year, *Dussehra*, which is like Thanksgiving, Christmas, Hallowe'en and New Year's rolled into one. *Dussehra* lasts for ten days. Schools close for about three weeks around this time.

Every house is shined and polished for *Dussehra*. In the villages, walls are whitewashed, and fresh mud floors are laid down. Children get toys made of colored sugar. Everyone is dressed up. Even the family animals are painted with gay designs.

The festival of Dussehra is devoted to the young Prince Rama and his beautiful wife, the Princess Sita. Rama, it is thought, was the god Vishnu who came to earth as Prince Rama to rescue the earth from evil and married there the lovely Sita. So the story is told in the *Ramayana*, one of the great epic poems of India.

Every year the story of Rama and Sita is enacted during *Dussehra* in the *Ram Lila*, or Play of Rama. The Play of Rama tells how wicked demons pursued Rama and stole Sita away, and how monkeys helped Rama to rescue Sita.

The poorest village always manages to put on a performance of the *Ram Lila*. All the villagers know the story and love it. They save the precious red and yellow silk costumes and monkey masks of the actors from year to year. Some of the villagers dress up as devils and monkeys too.

Most of them like the last scene of the play best of all, when the demons are lined up to be shot. The demons are made of bamboo stuffed with fireworks. A hush always falls, and then loud cheers burst forth as Rama shoots the arrow that is the signal for the bamboo to be set on fire and for the fireworks to go off in glorious explosions.

Dussehra ends with a joyous ceremony, the festival of lights called *Divali*, dedicated to Lakshmi, the goddess of wealth and beauty.

For Lakshmi's festival, each household prepares *chirags*, red saucers filled with oil and a bit of cotton wick. People outline their houses, gardens, wells, gates, and paths with the little lamps. At

Twinkling lamps on a garden wall will bring good luck on Divali.

Information Service of India, New York

Wishes will come true if these lamps stay lit till out of sight.

twilight the lamps are lit, and even the humblest village looks like a fairyland. One of the purposes of the lights is to guide Lakshmi to homes where she can bring gifts of good fortune.

The children go down to the Ganges and float other *chirags* down the river. Each child makes a wish as his tiny lamp floats off. If the lamp remains lit until it is out of sight, he knows his wish will come true.

In the cities electric light bulbs, like Christmas tree lights, may take the place of the little oil lamps, but the celebration is the same.

In Calcutta, *Dussehra* is known as *Durga Puja*. *Puja* means worship, and *Durga* is another name for Kali, the local goddess, after whom Calcutta is named.

Durga is represented as a rather terrifying black image wearing a necklace of skulls, but she, too, is supposed to fight a battle with evil for the good of mankind. People throw images of Durga into the river for good luck. Sometimes they even jump in after the images themselves. They are supposed to have particularly good luck if they are sprinkled by water splashing from the holy images. They figure the closer they get, the better chance they have of being splashed.

T. S. Satyan, Life Magazine © Time Inc.

Vinoba Bhave and his followers walk along the Ganges plain asking farmers to share their land with others.

11. River of Hope

Like Gandhi, his follower Vinoba Bhave believes in action, not talk.

When the new Indian government wanted to give poor farmers enough land to make them self-supporting, Bhave offered to help. He is a very old man, but he walks along the banks of the Ganges, asking farmers who have more land than they need to give some of it—free—to those who have none at all.

"If you had four sons and a fifth was born," Bhave says, "you would give that son a share of what you had, wouldn't you? Consider me your fifth son, and give me his share for the poor."

Someone figured that Bhave has walked the equivalent of twice across the United States. He has obtained 2,000,000 acres of land for redistribution, 90 per cent of it on the Ganges plain.

But important though Bhave's efforts are, they cannot solve the problem of poverty in the Ganges villages.

So many people are being born there that the food supply cannot catch up. More than half of those now living on the Ganges plain are younger than 20 years old. Far fewer children die of disease than formerly. Most can expect to live at least eighteen years longer than they would have if they had been born fifteen years ago. Adults live longer, too, thanks to modern medicine and better sanitation. With so many new mouths to feed, every bit of land must be made to yield as much as possible.

Crop failure brings tragedy. When monsoon rains were poor in recent years, terrible suffering followed. Famine stalked the villages. Farm families lived on roots and leaves. People and cattle wandered helplessly in search of water. Thousands died, and millions nearly starved. Tons of emergency food had to be flown in from the United States and other parts of the world.

When a good monsoon finally broke the drought, the Indian government vowed there would never be such misery again. It doubled the amount of money it was spending to help farmers and their families and increased its efforts to teach them to help themselves.

Like other Indian farmers, the Ganges villagers have always been hard-working and skillful. But they lack modern machinery, and many hesitate to try new ways.

There are encouraging signs of change. Hundreds of thousands of new deep tube wells are being dug to replace the old shallow wells which would dry up too fast.

The government is building some of the world's greatest dams. The Rihand Dam, built with help from the United States, will create the biggest man-made lake in Asia. It contains enough concrete to build all the pyramids of Egypt. The Damodar Valley project, also being built with

Information Service of India, New York

Towering Rihand Dam brings water and electricity to farmers.

American help, is modeled after the Tennessee Valley Authority. It will irrigate more than a million and a half acres, as well as control floods and provide power.

Experts from many lands are showing farmers how new types of seeds can give them better crops of rice, corn, and wheat. American Peace

92

Corps workers go into the villages to demonstrate new methods of farming and sanitation. The Ford Foundation, has projects to show farmers that money spent on better seeds, fertilizer, machinery, and irrigation can double and triple the value of their crops. The Rockefeller Foundation, another American private agency, has worked with Indians to develop new high-yielding seed strains.

The Indian government has created eight new agricultural universities. The University of Illinois helped to set up one of them. Graduates teach farming in the villages. Incidentally, these young people probably help break down caste prejudice,

Modern farming equipment will one day replace the traditional wooden plow and oxen.

for when they work in the fields, they pay no attention to caste differences.

Farmers also go to school to learn to read and write. Three fourths of all Indians still do not read, but if they want to farm the modern way, they must know how to read instructions.

Most important of all, old habits of thinking are changing. The people of the Ganges plain, like their brothers and sisters elsewhere in India, have always been uncomplaining. Now they are learning that patience is not enough. They see that it is possible to make life better, if not for themselves, then certainly for their children. They realize that the Ganges may be like a mother to them, but even the best mother needs help sometimes to get her work done.

Index

VIOLET WEINGARTEN was born in San Francisco and grew up in New York City. After graduating from Cornell University, she worked as a newspaper reporter. Her assignments included everything from royal visits and murder trials to bagpipe-playing concerts. Now she works with her husband, Victor, in their public relations office. She has written innumerable pamphlets as well as the scripts for several prize-winning motion pictures produced by Mr. Weingarten.

A few years ago, the Weingartens with their two daughters, Jan and Kathy, took a long European trip. They traveled by plane, ship, train, bus, car, gondola, cogtrain, subway, trolley, helicopter and donkey. On their return, Mrs. Weingarten and Kathy, then 13, wrote a book about their travels. In addition, Mrs. Weingarten has written three Rivers of the World books for Garrard: *The Nile*, *The Jordan*, and *The Ganges*.

The Weingartens' home is deep in the woods outside Mount Kisco, New York.

Calogero Cascio from Rapho Guillumette